KEEP IT SIMPLE: THE ESSENCE OF LEADERSHIP FOR BUSINESS SUCCESS

FIDELIS GOMES

TABLE OF CONTENTS

ACKNOWLEDGMENT

This book is dedicated with love to my daughter, Josephine, whose unwavering belief in me has been my guiding light. To my beloved wife, Catherine, your endless support and patience have been my greatest strength—I couldn't have done this without you. To my dear parents, now watching over me from heaven, your love and teachings continue to inspire me every day. A heartfelt thanks to Lucas Dawson from Writers Publishing Lab, whose guidance and expertise have been instrumental in bringing this book to life.

My journey as an author has been deeply shaped by the wisdom and inspiration I have gathered from countless books and authors, whose thoughtful words have motivated me. I would like to take this opportunity to express my profound gratitude to each of them—thank you!

This journey would not have been possible without each of you. Thank you from my heart.

INTRODUCTION

"Simplicity is the ultimate sophistication."

— LEONARDO DA VINCI

In the relentless pace of today's business world, leadership has become a labyrinth of complexities. Layers of bureaucracy, rigid hierarchies, and convoluted strategies have transformed what should be a straightforward endeavor into an overwhelming maze. Leaders, striving to navigate this complexity, often lose sight of what truly matters: the people they lead and the goals they aim to achieve. The result? Disengaged teams, inefficient operations, and a widespread crisis of trust.

Modern leadership is plagued by overcomplication. Research from Gallup reveals that only 21% of employees worldwide feel engaged at work. This alarming statistic underscores a critical issue: traditional leadership models, with their excessive focus on control and compliance, are failing. Instead of fostering collaboration and innovation, they create barriers that stifle creativity and erode morale. It's a system that prioritizes processes over people, perpetuating a cycle of inefficiency and dissatisfaction. Disengaged employees cost the global economy approximately $7.8 trillion annually, according to Gallup's 2022 State of the Global Workplace report.

1

This staggering figure highlights the urgent need for leaders to rethink their approach.

Consider this: a study by Deloitte found that organizations with simple, streamlined structures are 12% more likely to achieve higher performance. Yet, many leaders cling to outdated paradigms, equating complexity with sophistication and control with effectiveness. They rely on micromanagement, rigid protocols, and top-down decision-making, believing these approaches will yield results. In reality, these practices often lead to burnout, turnover, and stagnation. According to the American Institute of Stress, workplace stress costs U.S. employers over $300 billion annually in absenteeism, turnover, and reduced productivity. Much of this stress stems from overly complex systems and lack of clarity in leadership.

But what if there was a better way? What if leadership could be reimagined as a force for empowerment rather than control? Enter the concept of simplicity. Simplicity in leadership is not about reducing ambition or compromising on quality. Instead, it's about cutting through the noise to focus on what truly matters: clear communication, meaningful relationships, and shared purpose. Research by McKinsey & Company suggests that organizations prioritizing simplicity in their operations and leadership models see a 25% increase in employee satisfaction and a 30% boost in efficiency. This is because simplicity fosters an environment where teams can thrive, free from unnecessary barriers and distractions.

Leaders who embrace simplicity understand the value of trust and empowerment. They delegate effectively, encourage open dialogue, and create a culture of accountability. A Harvard Business Review study found that employees working under empowering leaders were 67% more engaged and 20% more innovative than those in traditional, hierarchical setups. By focusing on clear goals and streamlined processes, these leaders unlock their team's potential, driving both individual and organizational success.

The path to simplicity requires a shift in mindset. Leaders must unlearn the belief that complexity equates to control and recognize that true effectiveness lies in clarity and connection. Simplicity is not just a leadership strategy—it's a philosophy that transforms organizations, nurtures talent, and builds a foundation for sustainable success.

THE CASE FOR SIMPLICITY

At its core, simplicity in leadership is about focusing on what truly matters: trust, respect, empathy, and service. It's about cutting through the noise and honing in on the principles that drive success. As Albert Einstein famously said, "Everything should be made as simple as possible, but not simpler." This philosophy is especially relevant in leadership, where the ability to distill complex challenges into clear, actionable strategies can mean the difference between success and failure.

Simplicity in leadership doesn't mean oversimplifying or ignoring nuance; it's about identifying and prioritizing the essentials. Effective leaders understand that complexity often leads to confusion, inefficiency, and frustration. By eliminating unnecessary layers of bureaucracy and focusing on clear goals, leaders can inspire their teams to work smarter, not harder. This approach fosters a culture of clarity and alignment, where everyone understands their role and how it contributes to the organization's mission.

Simplicity is not about doing less; it's about doing what matters most. When leaders embrace simplicity, they create an environment where teams can thrive. Employees feel valued and supported, communication becomes more transparent, and decision-making is more efficient. The benefits are tangible: better outcomes, lower costs, and happier teams. In fact, a study by McKinsey & Company found that organizations with simpler structures and processes are 30% more likely to outperform their competitors. This underscores the power of simplicity in driving both employee engagement and business success.

Take the example of Southwest Airlines. Known for its no-frills approach, the company has consistently outperformed competitors by prioritizing simplicity. From streamlined operations to a people-first culture, Southwest's leadership philosophy proves that simplicity can be a powerful driver of success. Herb Kelleher, the airline's co-founder, famously stated, "The business of business is people. Yesterday, today, and forever." By focusing on people and eliminating unnecessary complexity, Southwest has built a brand synonymous with reliability and customer satisfaction.

Southwest's success is rooted in its ability to make complex systems work seamlessly. For instance, the airline operates with a single aircraft type, the Boeing 737, which simplifies maintenance, training, and scheduling. This decision, while seemingly straightforward, has profound implications for operational efficiency and cost management. Additionally, Southwest's boarding process is designed for speed and simplicity, allowing the airline to maintain a rapid turnaround time that maximizes profitability.

These choices highlight how simplicity, when strategically implemented, can become a competitive advantage.

Another key aspect of simplicity in leadership is effective communication. Leaders who prioritize simplicity in their messaging ensure that their vision and goals are understood at every level of the organization. Research by Gallup reveals that employees who feel connected to their organization's mission are 27% more likely to perform at a high level. Clear, concise communication fosters this connection, enabling teams to align their efforts and focus on shared objectives. When leaders articulate their vision in straightforward terms, they eliminate ambiguity and empower their teams to act with confidence and purpose.

Simplicity also extends to decision-making. In today's fast-paced business environment, leaders are often faced with an overwhelming array of choices. The ability to cut through the noise and focus on the most critical decisions is a hallmark of effective leadership. Jeff Bezos, the founder of Amazon, advocates for a "two-way door" approach to decision-making, where reversible decisions are made quickly to maintain momentum. This philosophy reflects the importance of simplicity in avoiding analysis paralysis and fostering a culture of agility and innovation.

Moreover, simplicity in leadership has a profound impact on employee well-being. A workplace culture that emphasizes clear expectations, streamlined processes, and open communication reduces stress and enhances job satisfaction. According to the American Psychological Association, employees in supportive work environments are more likely to report higher levels of job satisfaction and lower levels of burnout. By removing unnecessary complexities, leaders create a space where employees can focus on meaningful work without being bogged down by inefficiencies or misunderstandings.

Consider the example of Apple under the leadership of Steve Jobs. Jobs was a master of simplicity, both in product design and organizational strategy. His insistence on simplicity led to iconic products like the iPhone, which revolutionized the tech industry by combining multiple functionalities into a single, user-friendly device. Internally, Jobs streamlined Apple's product lineup, focusing only on a few key products rather than spreading resources thin across numerous projects. This focus allowed Apple to allocate its resources effectively and maintain a high standard of quality and innovation.

Simplicity in leadership also fosters a culture of empowerment. When processes and expectations are clear, employees are more likely to take initiative and make decisions confidently. This empowerment not only boosts morale but also drives innovation, as team members feel encouraged to experiment and contribute ideas without fear of failure. Leaders who embrace simplicity recognize that their role is to serve as facilitators, removing obstacles and providing the tools and support their teams need to succeed.

Simplicity in leadership is a powerful principle that drives trust, respect, empathy, and service. By focusing on what truly matters, leaders can create an environment where teams thrive, communication flourishes, and decision-making is efficient. Whether through examples like Southwest Airlines' streamlined operations or Apple's focus on user-friendly innovation, the benefits of simplicity are evident. As Einstein's timeless wisdom reminds us, the art of simplicity lies in making things as straightforward as possible, without compromising on quality or effectiveness. Leaders who master this art will find themselves better equipped to navigate the complexities of today's business world while inspiring their teams to achieve extraordinary results.

SHIFTING THE FOCUS

The transition from complexity to simplicity requires a fundamental shift in mindset. It's about moving away from the command-and-control model of leadership and embracing a more collaborative, servant-oriented approach. Servant leadership, a concept popularized by Robert K. Greenleaf in the 1970s, is rooted in the idea that leaders exist to serve their teams. This approach prioritizes the needs of employees, empowering them to perform at their best.

Servant leadership is not just a feel-good philosophy; it's a proven strategy for success. A study published in the *Journal of Business Ethics* found that organizations led by servant leaders experienced higher employee satisfaction, increased innovation, and improved financial performance. By putting people first, these leaders create a culture of trust and respect that drives long-term success.

Consider the case of Satya Nadella, CEO of Microsoft. When Nadella took the helm in 2014, Microsoft was struggling with internal silos and a stagnant culture. Through a servant leadership approach, Nadella focused on fostering empathy, collaboration, and continuous learning. Under his leadership, Microsoft's market value has more than tripled, proving that simplicity and a people-first mindset can lead to extraordinary results.

WHAT TO EXPECT IN THIS BOOK

This book is a roadmap for leaders who aspire to simplify their approach and achieve sustainable success. It challenges the conventional wisdom that leadership must be complex to be effective, offering an alternative perspective rooted in timeless values and practical strategies. Through real-world examples and actionable insights, you'll learn how to:

Embrace Servant Leadership: Discover how to put your team's needs first, removing obstacles and providing the support they need to excel.

Build Trust and Respect: Learn how to foster a culture of transparency and accountability, where employees feel valued and empowered.

Practice Empathy: Understand the emotional needs of your team and create an inclusive environment where everyone can thrive.

Streamline Operations: Eliminate unnecessary layers of management and simplify decision-making processes to improve efficiency.

Focus on Outcomes: Shift your attention from rigid protocols to meaningful results, prioritizing what truly matters.

Each chapter delves into a specific aspect of simplified leadership, providing practical tools and real-life examples to guide you on your journey. From dismantling toxic management structures to fostering a sales-driven culture, this book equips you with the knowledge and strategies to lead with clarity and purpose.

A CALL TO ACTION

Leadership is not about titles or authority; it's about impact. As you embark on this journey, I challenge you to reflect on your own leadership style. Are you prioritizing people over processes? Are you creating an environment where your team can thrive? If the answer is no, it's time to make a change.

The path to effective leadership is not complicated; it's simple. By focusing on trust, respect, empathy, and service, you can build a thriving organization that achieves extraordinary results. As Steve Jobs once said, "Simple can be harder than complex: You have to work hard to get your thinking clean to make it simple. But it's worth it in the end because once you get there, you can move mountains."

This book is your guide to moving mountains. *Let's begin!*

CHAPTER 1

SERVING LEADERSHIP
THE HEART OF SIMPLICITY

"Leadership is not about being in charge. It is about taking care of those in your charge."

— SIMON SINEK

WHAT IS SERVING LEADERSHIP?

At its core, serving leadership is a philosophy that flips the traditional leadership model on its head. Instead of focusing on authority and control, serving leadership prioritizes the needs of the team, empowering them to achieve their full potential. This approach fosters collaboration, trust, and long-term success by placing the well-being of the team above the leader's personal ambitions.

The traditional "command and control" model of leadership often emphasizes hierarchy, with the leader positioned at the top. Leaders in such systems typically focus on issuing directives, maintaining control, and ensuring compliance. While this model may deliver short-term results, it often stifles creativity, discourages collaboration, and creates a culture of fear rather than trust. In contrast, serving leadership operates on a "support and empower" model, where the leader's role is to create an environment where their team can thrive. This shift requires humility, empathy, and a deep commitment to the growth of others.

Robert K. Greenleaf, who coined the term "servant leadership" in his 1970 essay, described it as "a philosophy and set of practices that enrich the lives of individuals, build better organizations, and ultimately create a more just and caring world." Serving leadership is not about relinquishing authority but about using it to serve the greater good of the team and organization. This principle aligns closely with the concept of emotional intelligence in leadership, which emphasizes self-awareness, empathy, and the ability to foster meaningful relationships.

One of the defining characteristics of serving leadership is its focus on the personal and professional growth of team members. Leaders who adopt this approach invest in their team's development, providing mentorship, resources, and opportunities for skill-building. For example, a serving leader might prioritize one-on-one coaching sessions to understand each team member's aspirations and challenges, tailoring their support to meet individual needs. This personalized approach not only builds trust but also boosts morale and engagement. Studies show that employees who feel supported by their leaders are 3.5 times more likely to be engaged at work, leading to higher productivity and job satisfaction.

Serving leadership also emphasizes the importance of shared decision-making. By involving team members in the decision-making process, leaders demonstrate respect for their perspectives and foster a sense of ownership. This collaborative approach encourages innovation, as team members feel empowered to contribute their ideas without fear of judgment.

A 2019 study by the Harvard Business Review found that organizations with inclusive decision-making processes experienced 30% higher profitability compared to those that relied solely on top-down directives.

Moreover, serving leadership has a ripple effect that extends beyond the workplace. By modeling compassion, integrity, and a commitment to service, leaders inspire their teams to adopt similar values in their interactions with colleagues, clients, and the community. This creates a culture of service that enhances the organization's reputation and strengthens its impact. For instance, companies known for their servant leadership practices, such as Southwest Airlines and Patagonia, consistently rank high in employee satisfaction and customer loyalty.

However, serving leadership is not without its challenges. It requires a high degree of self-awareness and emotional resilience, as leaders must balance their team's needs with organizational goals. It also demands a willingness to embrace vulnerability, acknowledging that leadership is not about having all the answers but about fostering an environment where collective wisdom can flourish. Despite these challenges, the long-term benefits of serving leadership far outweigh the initial discomfort of adopting this mindset.

In today's rapidly changing world, where adaptability and innovation are crucial, serving leadership offers a sustainable path to success. By prioritizing the well-being and growth of their teams, leaders can cultivate a resilient and high-performing workforce. As Greenleaf aptly stated, "The servant-leader is servant first. It begins with the natural feeling that one wants to serve, to serve first." This timeless philosophy reminds us that true leadership is not about power or prestige but about the profound impact we can have on others.

KEY PRINCIPLES OF SERVING LEADERSHIP

1. Removing Obstacles That Hinder Employee Performance

A serving leader identifies and removes barriers that prevent their team from performing at their best. These obstacles can be organizational, such as outdated processes, or personal, such as a lack of confidence. By addressing these challenges, leaders enable their teams to focus on their goals without unnecessary distractions.

For example, consider a team struggling with inefficient communication tools. A serving leader would prioritize implementing better solutions, such as collaborative software, to streamline workflows. This proactive approach not only enhances productivity but also demonstrates a commitment to the team's success.

2. Providing Necessary Resources and Guidance

Serving leaders understand that their teams need access to the right resources to succeed. This includes everything from training and development opportunities to the tools required for their roles. Leaders who invest in their team's growth and development often see a significant return in terms of loyalty, innovation, and performance.

A 2019 study by LinkedIn revealed that 94% of employees would stay longer at a company if it invested in their learning and development. This statistic underscores the importance of providing resources that empower employees to grow both personally and professionally.

3. Leading by Example to Foster Respect and Trust

The foundation of serving leadership is leading by example. A leader's actions set the tone for the entire organization. By demonstrating integrity, accountability, and a strong work ethic, serving leaders inspire their teams to embody these values.

In his book *Leaders Eat Last*, Simon Sinek emphasizes the importance of leaders creating a "circle of safety" where team members feel valued and protected. This environment fosters trust and encourages open communication, enabling teams to collaborate effectively.

REAL-LIFE EXAMPLES

1. Southwest Airlines

Southwest Airlines is a shining example of serving leadership in action. Herb Kelleher, the company's co-founder, believed that treating employees well would lead to exceptional customer service. He famously stated, "Your employees come first. And if you treat your employees right, guess what? Your customers come back, and that makes your shareholders happy."

This philosophy has been instrumental in Southwest's success. By prioritizing employee satisfaction, the company has maintained high levels of customer loyalty and profitability. In 2022, Southwest ranked among the top airlines for customer satisfaction, a testament to its commitment to serving leadership.

2. Starbucks

Under the leadership of Howard Schultz, Starbucks embraced serving leadership as a core principle. Schultz focused on creating a supportive and inclusive culture for employees, whom he referred to as "partners." This approach included offering benefits like healthcare and stock options, even for part-time workers.

Schultz's dedication to serving leadership helped Starbucks grow from a single coffee shop in Seattle to a global powerhouse. His belief that "when you're surrounded by people who share a passionate commitment around a common purpose, anything is possible" reflects the essence of serving leadership.

3. Patagonia

Patagonia's founder, Yvon Chouinard, built the company on the principles of serving leadership. By prioritizing environmental sustainability and employee well-being, Patagonia has created a loyal customer base and a thriving workforce. The company's "Let My People Go Surfing" policy, which allows employees to take breaks for outdoor activities, exemplifies its commitment to serving leadership.

Chouinard's philosophy demonstrates that businesses can succeed while prioritizing the needs of their employees and the planet. In 2022, Patagonia announced that its profits would be reinvested into fighting climate change, further solidifying its reputation as a purpose-driven organization.

ACTION STEPS FOR LEADERS

1. Identify and Eliminate Barriers to Team Success

The first step in embracing serving leadership is identifying the obstacles that hinder your team's performance. This requires active listening and open communication. Regularly seek feedback from your team to understand their challenges and needs.

Once you've identified these barriers, take proactive steps to address them. For example, if team members feel overwhelmed by unrealistic deadlines, work with them to create a more manageable schedule. By demonstrating your commitment to their well-being, you build trust and loyalty.

2. Create Systems for Consistent Feedback and Support

Effective serving leadership requires ongoing communication. Establish systems for regular feedback, such as one-on-one meetings or anonymous surveys. Use this feedback to make informed decisions and provide the support your team needs.

In addition to feedback, offer mentorship and guidance. A 2020 report by the Association for Talent Development found that employees with access to mentorship programs are 67% more likely to stay with their organizations. By investing in your team's growth, you create a culture of continuous improvement and mutual respect.

3. Foster a Culture of Empathy and Inclusion

Empathy is a cornerstone of serving leadership. Make an effort to understand your team members' perspectives and show genuine concern for their well-being. This includes recognizing and celebrating their achievements, as well as supporting them during challenging times.

Inclusion is equally important. Create an environment where everyone feels valued and respected, regardless of their background or role. A 2021 study by McKinsey & Company found that diverse teams are 35% more likely to outperform their peers. By fostering inclusion, you not only strengthen your team but also drive innovation and success.

4. Lead with Purpose and Vision

Serving leaders inspire their teams by articulating a clear purpose and vision. This gives team members a sense of direction and motivation. According to a 2018 survey by Gallup, employees who feel connected to their organization's mission are 27% more likely to stay and 21% more productive.

Ensure that your vision aligns with your team's values and goals. Communicate it consistently and passionately, and involve your team in shaping its execution. By leading with purpose, you create a shared sense of commitment and drive.

Serving leadership is not a fleeting trend but a timeless approach that fosters trust, collaboration, and sustainable success. It is rooted in the principle that leadership is about service rather than authority, emphasizing the importance of empowering others to achieve their best. By putting the needs of your team first, removing obstacles, providing resources, and leading by example, you can create an environment where everyone thrives. This approach not only builds stronger relationships within the organization but also enhances overall productivity and morale.

One of the key aspects of serving leadership is its ability to cultivate trust. Trust is the foundation of any successful team, and leaders who prioritize the well-being of their members demonstrate genuine care and commitment. When employees feel valued and supported, they are more likely to engage deeply with their work and contribute to the organization's goals. Research from Gallup shows that teams with high levels of trust report 50% higher productivity and 40% lower turnover rates. These statistics highlight the tangible benefits of adopting a leadership style centered on service and empathy.

Serving leadership also encourages collaboration by breaking down traditional hierarchical barriers. Leaders who actively involve their team members in decision-making processes foster a sense of ownership and accountability. This inclusivity not only generates innovative ideas but also strengthens the collective resolve to overcome challenges. In a Harvard Business Review study, organizations that embraced collaborative leadership saw a 30% increase in their ability to adapt to market changes, showcasing the adaptability and resilience that serving leadership can bring.

Moreover, serving leadership emphasizes the removal of obstacles that hinder progress. Leaders who proactively identify and address these barriers empower their teams to focus on what truly matters. Whether it's streamlining workflows, addressing interpersonal conflicts, or ensuring access to necessary tools and resources, serving leaders pave the way for their teams to excel. This hands-on approach reflects a deep understanding of the challenges employees face and a commitment to resolving them.

Providing resources is another critical component of serving leadership. Leaders who invest in the growth and development of their team members create a culture of continuous improvement. This investment can take many forms, from offering professional development opportunities to mentoring individuals on their career paths. Studies from the Center for Creative Leadership indicate that organizations with strong leadership development programs outperform their peers by 15% in profitability. By prioritizing the growth of their teams, serving leaders not only enhance individual capabilities but also contribute to the long-term success of their organizations.

Leading by example is perhaps the most powerful way to inspire and influence others. Actions speak louder than words, and serving leaders model the values and behaviors they wish to see in their teams. This authenticity fosters a culture of accountability and integrity, where team members feel motivated to emulate their leader's example. As John Quincy Adams famously said, "If your actions inspire others to dream more, learn more, do more, and become more, you are a leader." Serving leadership embodies this sentiment, creating a ripple effect that extends far beyond the immediate team.

As Simon Sinek reminds us, "Leadership is not about being in charge. It is about taking care of those in your charge." This philosophy underscores the essence of serving leadership, where the focus shifts from self-interest to collective well-being. Embracing this approach requires humility, empathy, and a genuine desire to make a positive impact. Yet, the rewards are immeasurable: a cohesive team, a thriving organization, and a legacy of leadership that inspires others to follow suit.

Serving leadership proves that simplicity, authenticity, and purpose are the keys to unlocking the full potential of your team and organization. It challenges conventional notions of leadership by prioritizing service over authority and collaboration over control. By adopting this timeless approach, you not only lead with integrity but also create an enduring foundation for success that benefits everyone involved.

CHAPTER 2

TRUST AND RESPECT
THE FOUNDATION OF LEADERSHIP

"Trust is the glue of life. It's the most essential ingredient in effective communication. It's the foundational principle that holds all relationships."

— STEPHEN COVEY

TRUST AND RESPECT – THE FOUNDATION OF LEADERSHIP

Leadership is more than a title or a position; it is a relationship built on trust and respect. These two principles form the bedrock of effective leadership, enabling teams to thrive and organizations to achieve their goals. Without trust and respect, even the most skilled leaders struggle to inspire loyalty, foster collaboration, or drive sustainable success.

Trust is the glue that holds a team together. According to Stephen M.R. Covey, author of The Speed of Trust, "Trust is the one thing that changes everything." It fosters an environment where individuals feel safe to share ideas, take risks, and contribute their best efforts without fear of judgment or failure. When employees trust their leaders, they are more likely to remain engaged, productive, and committed to the organization's vision.

Research from Edelman's Trust Barometer reveals that companies with high levels of trust outperform their competitors, boasting higher employee retention, customer loyalty, and profitability.

Building trust requires consistency, transparency, and authenticity. Leaders must follow through on their promises, communicate openly, and demonstrate integrity in their actions. It is not enough to speak about values; a leader must live them. For instance, when a leader admits to a mistake and takes responsibility, it not only humanizes them but also strengthens trust within the team. Trust is cultivated over time, but it can be lost in an instant through dishonesty or inconsistency.

Respect is equally vital. It is the acknowledgment of each individual's inherent worth, abilities, and contributions. Leaders who respect their team members foster a culture of mutual appreciation and inclusivity. This respect encourages diversity of thought, innovation, and collaboration. As former U.S. President Theodore Roosevelt aptly said, "People don't care how much you know until they know how much you care." Respecting your team means listening to their concerns, valuing their input, and empowering them to grow.

Respect also plays a crucial role in conflict resolution. In high-stakes environments, disagreements are inevitable. Leaders who approach conflicts with respect for all parties involved create opportunities for constructive dialogue and resolution. This approach minimizes resentment and strengthens team cohesion.

Trust and respect are deeply interconnected. A leader cannot earn respect without first establishing trust, and trust cannot flourish in the absence of respect. Together, they form a virtuous cycle that reinforces positive relationships and organizational health. Consider a workplace where employees trust their leader to act in their best interests and respect their contributions. Such an environment breeds loyalty, boosts morale, and drives performance.

In a world where leadership is increasingly scrutinized, trust and respect have never been more important. Leaders who prioritize these values not only elevate their teams but also set the standard for ethical and effective leadership. By building relationships on this foundation, they inspire others to follow, collaborate, and excel, creating a legacy of success that transcends their tenure.

THE IMPORTANCE OF TRUST IN LEADERSHIP

Trust is the invisible thread that connects leaders to their teams. According to a study by Edelman's Trust Barometer, 61% of employees believe that trust in their leadership is critical for their job satisfaction and performance. When trust is present, it creates a positive work environment where individuals feel safe to express their ideas, take risks, and innovate. Conversely, broken trust can lead to disengagement, high turnover rates, and inefficiency.

For example, a 2021 Gallup survey revealed that organizations with high-trust environments experience 50% lower employee turnover and 21% higher profitability. These statistics highlight how trust directly impacts organizational performance. Leaders who prioritize trust empower their teams to reach their full potential, fostering a culture of accountability and mutual respect.

On the flip side, the consequences of broken trust can be devastating. Employees who feel betrayed or unsupported by their leaders are more likely to disengage, leading to decreased productivity. A study by the Society for Human Resource Management (SHRM) found that 58% of employees who leave their jobs cite a lack of trust in leadership as a significant factor. This underscores the need for leaders to cultivate and maintain trust to ensure long-term organizational success.

BUILDING AND MAINTAINING TRUST

Building trust requires intentionality and consistency. It is not something that can be demanded; it must be earned through actions that align with words. Two critical components of trust-building are transparency and accountability.

Transparency involves openly sharing goals, decisions, and challenges with your team. When leaders communicate honestly, they create a culture of openness that encourages collaboration. For instance, during the COVID-19 pandemic, organizations that maintained transparent communication about their challenges and strategies reported higher employee morale. A survey by McKinsey & Company found that 87% of employees valued transparency in leadership during uncertain times.

Accountability is equally vital. Leaders who follow through on their commitments demonstrate reliability and integrity. According to a Harvard Business Review article, accountability is one of the top traits employees seek in their leaders. Simple actions, such as meeting deadlines, admitting mistakes, and taking responsibility for outcomes, go a long way in building trust. When leaders hold themselves accountable, they set a standard for their teams to do the same.

THE ROLE OF RESPECT IN LEADERSHIP

While trust forms the foundation of leadership, respect strengthens its structure, acting as the glue that binds teams together and drives them toward shared success. Respect in leadership is about valuing diverse perspectives, recognizing individual contributions, and treating everyone with dignity. A leader who respects their team fosters an inclusive environment where everyone feels valued, heard, and empowered to contribute their best.

Research consistently highlights the transformative power of respect in leadership. A study by Deloitte reveals that inclusive teams outperform their peers by 80% in team-based assessments. This finding underscores the role of respect in driving collaboration, innovation, and productivity. When leaders prioritize respect, they create an atmosphere where team members feel safe to share ideas, take calculated risks, and challenge the status quo, all of which are critical for organizational growth.

Valuing diverse perspectives is a cornerstone of respectful leadership. In today's interconnected world, teams often comprise individuals from various cultural, professional, and personal backgrounds. Leaders who actively seek out and consider these diverse viewpoints gain access to a broader range of ideas and solutions, enhancing decision-making and problem-solving. For instance, a study by Boston Consulting Group found that companies with diverse management teams experience 19% higher revenue due to innovation. This statistic highlights how respect for diversity is not just a moral imperative but also a strategic advantage in a competitive marketplace.

Respectful leadership also involves recognizing individual contributions and celebrating successes, no matter how small. Employees who feel that their efforts are acknowledged and appreciated are more likely to remain engaged and motivated. Gallup's research indicates that employees who feel recognized are 4.6 times more likely to perform their best work. This recognition fosters a sense of pride and ownership, encouraging team members to go above and beyond in their roles.

Balancing authority with approachability is another critical aspect of respectful leadership. Leaders who maintain clear boundaries while remaining approachable create a culture of trust and open communication. This balance ensures that employees feel comfortable sharing their ideas or concerns without fear of judgment or retribution. A 2021 report by Catalyst highlights that employees with approachable leaders are 72% more likely to be highly engaged in their work. Such leaders inspire loyalty and commitment, reducing turnover and creating a stable, high-performing team.

Moreover, respect in leadership extends to how leaders handle conflicts and setbacks. Leaders who approach disagreements with empathy and a willingness to listen demonstrate that they value their team members as individuals, not just as contributors to organizational goals. This approach not only resolves issues more effectively but also strengthens relationships and reinforces a culture of mutual respect.

Ultimately, respect is not just a leadership quality—it is a leadership necessity. By valuing diversity, recognizing contributions, and balancing authority with approachability, leaders can create an environment where trust thrives, innovation flourishes, and teams achieve extraordinary results. Respect transforms leadership from a position of power into a practice of empowerment, laying the groundwork for sustainable success.

PRACTICAL APPLICATIONS

Understanding the importance of trust and respect is only the first step; applying these principles in daily leadership practices is where the real transformation occurs. Here are some practical strategies for building trust and respect within your team:

Trust-Building Exercises

Team-Building Activities: Activities such as problem-solving games or collaborative projects help strengthen relationships and build trust among team members.

Open Feedback Sessions: Encourage regular feedback exchanges where both leaders and team members can share constructive insights. This practice fosters transparency and mutual understanding.

Shared Goals and Achievements: Involve the team in setting goals and celebrate milestones together. This reinforces a sense of collective responsibility and trust.

Conflict Resolution Strategies Rooted in Respect

Active Listening: During conflicts, prioritize listening to all parties involved. Demonstrating empathy and understanding helps de-escalate tensions and shows respect for differing viewpoints.

Collaborative Problem-Solving: Encourage team members to work together to find solutions, emphasizing shared interests rather than individual positions.

Neutral Mediation: As a leader, act as a neutral mediator to facilitate discussions and ensure that all voices are heard and respected.

REAL-WORLD EXAMPLE: THE STARBUCKS LEADERSHIP MODEL

Starbucks' former CEO, Howard Schultz, is a prime example of a leader who exemplifies trust and respect. When Schultz returned as CEO in 2008, the company faced significant challenges, including declining sales and employee dissatisfaction. By focusing on transparency and respect, Schultz rebuilt the company's culture and restored its financial health.

Schultz implemented open forums where employees could voice their concerns and ideas. He also introduced initiatives to improve employee benefits, such as healthcare coverage and stock options. These actions demonstrated his commitment to earning trust and respecting his team, leading to increased employee engagement and customer satisfaction. Today, Starbucks is recognized as one of the most admired companies globally, thanks in part to Schultz's leadership principles.

Trust and respect are not just ideals; they are actionable principles that define effective leadership. By prioritizing transparency, accountability, and inclusivity, leaders can build strong, cohesive teams that drive organizational success. As Stephen Covey's quote reminds us, trust is the glue that holds relationships together. Combined with respect, it creates a leadership style that inspires loyalty, fosters collaboration, and achieves extraordinary results.

Leadership is a journey, not a destination. As you strive to lead with trust and respect, remember that every action, decision, and interaction contributes to the legacy you leave behind. The foundation you build today will shape the future of your team and organization for years to come.

CHAPTER 3

EMPATHY – UNDERSTANDING YOUR PEOPLE

"Leadership is not about being in charge. It is about taking care of those in your charge."

– SIMON SINEK

Empathy is the lifeblood of effective leadership, a skill that goes beyond technical expertise and managerial prowess. In a world where workplace dynamics are evolving rapidly, understanding your people— truly seeing them, hearing them, and valuing them—has never been more critical. Empathy bridges the gap between leaders and their teams, fostering trust, loyalty, and collaboration.

DEFINING EMPATHY IN LEADERSHIP

Empathy in leadership is the ability to recognize, understand, and address the emotional needs of employees. It goes beyond mere acknowledgment of feelings to actively considering and supporting the unique challenges and aspirations of each individual. This quality enables leaders to build deeper connections with their teams, fostering trust, loyalty, and a shared sense of purpose.

But what does empathy look like in practice? Consider an employee who is juggling work responsibilities with caregiving duties for a sick family member. An empathetic leader doesn't just express sympathy or offer well-meaning platitudes. Instead, they engage in meaningful dialogue to understand the employee's specific struggles. This could involve exploring options such as flexible working hours, remote work arrangements, or access to company-provided resources like counseling services or caregiver support programs. These tangible actions demonstrate that the leader values the employee's well-being as much as their productivity.

Empathy is not just a "soft skill"; it's a measurable driver of organizational success. According to studies conducted by the Center for Creative Leadership, empathy is directly linked to job performance. Employees who feel understood and supported by their leaders are 91% more likely to remain loyal to their organizations. This loyalty translates into higher retention rates, reduced recruitment costs, and a more engaged workforce. In an era where employee turnover and disengagement are costly challenges, empathy emerges as a vital tool for sustaining organizational health.

The broader implications of empathy in leadership are also significant. The American Institute of Stress reports that 83% of U.S. workers experience work-related stress, which costs businesses an estimated $300 billion annually in lost productivity. Stress-related issues, such as burnout and absenteeism, not only drain financial resources but also erode team morale and creativity. Empathetic leadership can act as a buffer against these pressures. By prioritizing emotional and mental health, leaders create an environment where employees feel safe, valued, and motivated to perform at their best.

Moreover, empathy enhances communication and collaboration within teams. When leaders actively listen to their employees and validate their experiences, it encourages open dialogue and fosters a culture of psychological safety. This, in turn, empowers employees to share ideas, voice concerns, and take calculated risks without fear of judgment or reprisal. As a result, organizations benefit from increased innovation and problem-solving capabilities.

Empathy also plays a critical role in addressing diversity and inclusion within the workplace. By understanding and appreciating the diverse backgrounds and perspectives of their team members, leaders can create equitable opportunities for growth and advancement. This not only strengthens organizational culture but also enhances overall performance, as diverse teams are proven to be more effective in achieving business goals.

In today's fast-paced, high-pressure work environments, empathy is more than just a moral imperative—it's a strategic advantage. Leaders who prioritize empathy are better equipped to navigate challenges, inspire their teams, and drive sustainable success. In essence, empathy transforms leadership from a transactional relationship into a transformational one, where employees and organizations thrive together.

WHY EMPATHY MATTERS

Empathy is more than a nice-to-have quality—it is a driving force behind morale, motivation, and loyalty. When leaders show genuine care, employees are more likely to invest their energy and creativity into their work. Research from Businessolver's State of Workplace Empathy Study found that 92% of employees believe empathy remains undervalued in their workplace, yet 96% agree that it is critical for employee retention. This highlights the disconnect between recognizing empathy's importance and effectively implementing it.

Empathy in leadership also promotes psychological safety, which is essential for high-performing teams. Employees who feel understood and valued are more likely to share ideas, take risks, and collaborate openly. This sense of safety reduces stress, improves job satisfaction, and ultimately boosts productivity. A 2021 study by Catalyst found that empathetic leaders positively impact employee engagement, with 61% of respondents reporting they were more innovative when their leaders demonstrated empathy.

Inclusivity and collaboration are other byproducts of empathetic leadership. A leader who takes the time to understand diverse perspectives fosters an environment where everyone feels valued. This inclusivity not only enhances team dynamics but also drives innovation. McKinsey's 2020 report on diversity found that companies with inclusive cultures are 25% more likely to achieve above-average profitability.

Consider the story of Satya Nadella, CEO of Microsoft, whose empathetic leadership has been pivotal in transforming the company's culture. Nadella's focus on emotional intelligence and his commitment to listening to employees have fostered a culture of collaboration and innovation. Under his leadership, Microsoft has seen its market value soar from $300 billion in 2014 to over $2 trillion today—a testament to the power of empathetic leadership. His approach proves that empathy is not just a moral choice but a strategic advantage in achieving sustainable success.

PRACTICAL TOOLS FOR EMPATHETIC LEADERSHIP

Empathy is a skill that can be developed with intentional effort. Leaders who invest in building emotional intelligence and practicing active listening create a ripple effect throughout their organizations. Here are some practical tools for empathetic leadership:

Active Listening Techniques

Active listening is a cornerstone of empathetic leadership, requiring full attention to the speaker, understanding their message, and responding thoughtfully. This skill goes beyond merely hearing words—it involves interpreting nonverbal cues, asking clarifying questions, and providing feedback that demonstrates understanding. For instance, leaders who actively listen avoid interrupting or formulating responses prematurely, opting instead to practice patience. They might use phrases such as, "What I'm hearing is…" or "It sounds like you're feeling…" to validate and affirm the speaker's experiences. These small but impactful actions build trust and create an environment where employees feel valued. A study published in the *Harvard Business Review* reveals that teams led by leaders who prioritize active listening outperform their peers by 23%, highlighting the tangible benefits of this skill. Additionally, active listening fosters innovation, as employees are more likely to share ideas when they feel genuinely heard.

BUILDING EMOTIONAL INTELLIGENCE (EQ)

Emotional intelligence (EQ)—the ability to recognize, understand, and manage emotions—is another critical component of empathetic leadership. Leaders with high EQ excel at navigating conflicts, inspiring teams, and fostering positive relationships. Daniel Goleman, a pioneer in emotional intelligence research, identifies five key components of EQ: self-awareness, self-regulation, motivation, empathy, and social skills. Developing EQ requires intentional effort. Leaders can practice mindfulness to enhance self-awareness, seek constructive feedback to identify blind spots, and engage in training programs focused on emotional intelligence. Research by TalentSmart shows that EQ accounts for 58% of performance in all job types, underscoring its importance. Furthermore, leaders with high EQ create psychologically safe workplaces, where employees are more engaged and productive, driving long-term organizational success.

Case Studies: Leaders Who Transformed Through Empathy

Empathy is not merely theoretical; it has real-world applications that lead to extraordinary outcomes. The following case studies illustrate how empathetic leadership can transform organizations:

Case Study 1: Arne Sorenson, Marriott International

When the COVID-19 pandemic devastated the hospitality industry, Arne Sorenson, then CEO of Marriott International, demonstrated exceptional empathy. In an emotional video message to employees, Sorenson openly acknowledged the hardships they were facing, including layoffs and reduced hours. His transparency and vulnerability resonated deeply with the Marriott team, fostering a sense of solidarity during an unprecedented crisis.

Despite the financial challenges, Sorenson prioritized employee welfare by maintaining health benefits for furloughed workers. His empathetic approach not only boosted morale but also reinforced Marriott's reputation as a company that cares for its people.

Case Study 2: Mary Barra, General Motors

Mary Barra, CEO of General Motors, exemplifies empathetic leadership by championing inclusivity and workplace culture. Under her guidance, GM has implemented initiatives to create a more inclusive environment, such as the "Speak Up for Safety" program, which encourages employees to voice concerns without fear of retribution.

Barra's empathetic leadership has contributed to GM's recognition as one of the "World's Most Ethical Companies" by the Ethisphere Institute. Her ability to connect with employees and understand their needs has been instrumental in fostering trust and collaboration.

BRINGING EMPATHY TO YOUR LEADERSHIP

As a leader, your ability to empathize with your team shapes the culture and success of your organization. It requires a commitment to listening, learning, and growing—both as an individual and as a steward of your team's well-being. Empathy is not a soft skill; it is a powerful tool that drives engagement, loyalty, and performance. When leaders show genuine concern for their team members, they create an environment where trust and collaboration thrive. This leads to greater innovation, productivity, and overall job satisfaction.

Empathy involves more than just understanding someone's emotions; it's about actively putting yourself in their shoes and recognizing their perspectives and challenges. It's about being present, acknowledging the feelings of others, and responding in a way that makes them feel heard and valued. By demonstrating empathy, you foster an atmosphere where employees feel safe to express their ideas, concerns, and even vulnerabilities, knowing they will be met with respect and understanding.

Start by asking yourself: How well do you understand your people? What steps can you take today to listen more actively and lead more compassionately? The answers to these questions will determine not only your success as a leader but also the resilience and prosperity of your organization. Empathetic leadership encourages open communication, reduces turnover, and enhances morale. When people feel valued, they are more likely to invest their energy and creativity into their work.

Incorporating empathy into your leadership style is a continuous journey. It requires self-awareness, patience, and the ability to adapt to the needs of your team. By prioritizing empathy, you not only foster a positive workplace culture but also set the foundation for sustainable growth and success.

CHAPTER 4

THE SIMPLEST SOLUTION – SALES

"The key to successful leadership today is influence, not authority."

– KEN BLANCHARD

Sales are the lifeblood of any business. They are not merely a function of an organization; they are the driving force that propels companies toward growth, stability, and innovation. Every decision made, every strategy formulated, and every process implemented in a successful company is ultimately geared toward one thing: increasing sales. This chapter will explore why sales drive everything, how sales success creates a ripple effect throughout an organization, and how leaders can simplify their approach to sales to ensure long-term success.

WHY SALES DRIVE EVERYTHING

At the heart of every thriving organization lies a strong sales engine. Sales are not just about closing deals or generating revenue; they are the direct link between an organization's products or services and the market's needs. A robust sales team acts as the bridge between a company's offerings and the customer, ensuring that the value being delivered resonates with the target audience. Strong sales reflect a company's ability to consistently meet and exceed customer expectations, and this value is what sustains the business in the long run.

A 2020 study by McKinsey & Company found that companies with strong sales performance saw 5 to 10 percent higher growth rates compared to their competitors. This shows that sales are not just important—they are essential to organizational health. Without consistent sales, businesses struggle to fund operations, pay employees, or invest in new projects. The lack of revenue creates a ripple effect, leading to cutbacks, loss of morale, and ultimately, stagnation. This is why sales are often considered the lifeblood of a company. Without them, even the best products or services will fail to reach their potential.

When sales are strong, however, the opposite happens. The organization becomes financially stable, which allows for more strategic investments in innovation, technology, and employee development. Sales drive everything, from product development to marketing to customer service. With a strong sales performance, businesses can allocate resources more effectively, ensuring that every department is aligned with the company's overarching goal of growth. By focusing on sales, leaders simplify decision-making because every decision can be aligned with the core goal of generating revenue and serving customers. Ultimately, a successful sales strategy lays the foundation for long-term sustainability and growth.

THE RIPPLE EFFECT OF SALES SUCCESS

Sales success is not confined to the sales department alone. When sales are strong, the entire organization benefits in ways that extend far beyond the bottom line. The financial stability generated by strong sales provides a foundation for innovation, growth, and strategic investments. With a steady stream of revenue, companies are able to reinvest in research and development, improve products, and explore new markets. This creates a cycle of reinvestment that propels the business forward, ensuring its long-term sustainability and competitiveness in the marketplace.

Take, for example, Apple Inc. The company's success in sales, particularly through its flagship iPhone product, has allowed it to fund some of the most groundbreaking innovations in technology. The iPhone's success has enabled Apple to expand into new areas like wearables, augmented reality, and even original content creation through its Apple TV+ platform. This expansion was not a result of a sudden windfall or a one-off product; rather, it was the outcome of consistent, high-performing sales that provided the financial cushion needed for risk-taking and innovation. Without strong sales, these innovations would not have been possible. In fact, Apple's sales success has been the key driver in its ability to push the boundaries of what's possible in technology, continually setting new standards for the industry.

But the ripple effect of sales success does not stop at financial stability. It also has a profound impact on employee morale, engagement, and confidence. When sales are strong, employees feel more secure in their jobs, which boosts productivity and engagement. In fact, a 2019 Gallup poll found that employees who work for companies with high sales performance are 25% more likely to be engaged in their work than those at companies with low sales performance. This heightened engagement stems from the sense of accomplishment employees feel when they know their contributions are directly tied to the company's success. It fosters a sense of pride and ownership, making employees more committed to the company's mission and more willing to go above and beyond in their roles.

Furthermore, strong sales often lead to improved compensation packages, bonuses, and career advancement opportunities, which further motivates employees to excel. When they see the tangible rewards of their hard work, it creates a positive feedback loop: strong sales lead to improved morale, which in turn leads to even stronger sales. This cycle reinforces the company's success, creating a thriving work environment where employees feel valued and motivated to contribute their best efforts.

The result is a company culture that is aligned, focused, and driven by the common goal of serving customers and achieving business success. Strong sales act as a catalyst for collaboration and innovation, as departments work together to meet customer needs and deliver exceptional products and services. This alignment not only enhances the customer experience but also strengthens the company's reputation in the marketplace, further fueling its sales success.

In conclusion, sales success is far more than just a financial boost for a company. It sets off a ripple effect that impacts every aspect of the organization, from innovation and growth to employee engagement and company culture. When sales thrive, the entire company thrives, creating a virtuous cycle of success that benefits employees, customers, and shareholders alike.

STRATEGIES FOR SALES-DRIVEN LEADERSHIP

As a leader, the key to fostering a sales-driven culture is to prioritize customer relationships and empower frontline teams. Sales are not just about pushing products; they are about understanding customer needs and providing solutions that create long-term value. This requires leaders to invest in training employees in salesmanship and interpersonal skills, ensuring that everyone in the organization understands the importance of sales and is equipped to contribute to the company's success. A sales-driven culture is built on the understanding that every team member plays a role in the customer experience and, ultimately, the business's growth.

One of the most effective ways to drive sales is to prioritize customer relationships. In today's competitive marketplace, customers have more choices than ever before. To stand out, businesses must focus on building trust and delivering exceptional customer service. A 2021 report by Salesforce found that 84% of customers say the experience a company provides is as important as its products or services. This means that salespeople need to be not just sellers, but trusted advisors who can guide customers toward the best solutions. A sales-driven leader recognizes the importance of listening to customers and tailoring the approach to meet their specific needs. By fostering a culture of empathy and customer-centricity, leaders can ensure that their teams are not only meeting sales targets but also creating lasting relationships with clients.

Training employees in salesmanship is essential for creating a sales-driven culture. This does not mean turning every employee into a professional salesperson, but rather equipping them with the skills to engage with customers effectively. Whether it's a customer service representative or a marketing professional, every employee should be able to understand customer needs and contribute to the sales process. Leaders must invest in continuous learning, offering regular training sessions that focus on both hard skills, like product knowledge, and soft skills, like active listening and relationship-building. A well-trained team can identify opportunities for upselling, cross-selling, and providing solutions that customers may not have initially considered, ultimately increasing sales revenue.

In addition to training, sales-driven leadership involves empowering frontline teams. These are the employees who interact with customers on a daily basis and have the most direct impact on sales. By giving them the tools, resources, and authority to make decisions, leaders can ensure that customer needs are met quickly and efficiently. According to a 2020 survey by McKinsey, companies that empower their frontline teams to make decisions see a 25% increase in customer satisfaction and a 15% increase in sales performance. Empowerment comes from trust and clear communication, allowing frontline employees to feel confident in their ability to solve problems and seize opportunities when they arise. This autonomy boosts morale and leads to more effective customer interactions, resulting in higher conversion rates and customer loyalty.

Leaders who prioritize sales-driven strategies understand that sales are not just a department—they are a mindset that permeates the entire organization. By fostering a culture of sales excellence, leaders create an environment where everyone is focused on delivering value to customers and driving the company's success. This mindset extends beyond the sales team and becomes part of the company's DNA. From the CEO to entry-level employees, everyone should feel responsible for the company's sales goals. Sales-driven leadership also means measuring success not just by revenue, but by customer satisfaction, repeat business, and long-term relationships. In this way, sales are not just a transaction—they are a reflection of the company's commitment to delivering value and fostering trust.

Ultimately, a sales-driven leader is one who recognizes that the sales process is not just about making a sale today but about creating a lasting impact on customers that will lead to continued business success in the future.

AVOIDING COMMON PITFALLS

While sales are crucial to business success, it is easy for organizations to overcomplicate their sales strategies. One of the most common pitfalls is adding unnecessary processes and layers of bureaucracy that slow down decision-making and hinder the sales team's ability to respond to customer needs quickly. This is especially true in larger organizations, where the desire to standardize and control processes can stifle creativity and innovation.

A report by the Harvard Business Review found that organizations with overly complex sales processes are 40% less likely to achieve their sales targets than those with streamlined, efficient processes. The key to avoiding this pitfall is to simplify sales strategies and focus on what truly matters: building relationships with customers and delivering value.

Leaders should also avoid the temptation to micromanage sales teams. While it is important to provide guidance and support, excessive oversight can create an environment of fear and mistrust. Salespeople who feel they are constantly being monitored are less likely to take risks or think creatively, which can ultimately hurt sales performance. Instead, leaders should focus on providing clear goals, offering support when needed, and trusting their teams to execute the sales strategy.

Another common mistake is focusing too much on short-term sales goals at the expense of long-term customer relationships. While it is important to meet quarterly or annual sales targets, organizations that prioritize short-term gains often find themselves sacrificing customer loyalty and satisfaction. In the long run, this can hurt the company's reputation and sales performance. A study by Bain & Company found that increasing customer retention by just 5% can lead to a 25% to 95% increase in profits. This highlights the importance of building lasting relationships with customers, rather than simply focusing on immediate sales.

Sales are the simplest solution to many of the challenges faced by businesses today. They drive everything, from organizational health to financial stability to employee morale. By focusing on sales, leaders can simplify decision-making and strategy, ensuring that every action taken is aligned with the goal of delivering value to customers. The ripple effect of sales success extends throughout the organization, creating a positive feedback loop that fuels innovation, growth, and a thriving company culture.

To foster a sales-driven culture, leaders must prioritize customer relationships, invest in employee training, and empower frontline teams. By avoiding common pitfalls such as overcomplicating sales strategies and focusing too much on short-term goals, businesses can create an environment where sales flourish, and success follows.

In the end, sales are not just about closing deals—they are about creating lasting value for customers and driving the success of the organization. By embracing a sales-driven approach, leaders can ensure that their businesses thrive in an increasingly competitive marketplace.

CHAPTER 5

UNNECESSARY LAYERS
THE COST OF COMPLEXITY

"Elegance is the only beauty that never fades."

– AUDREY HEPBURN

In a world that's constantly evolving, we often find ourselves adding layers to our processes, systems, and structures. It's as if we believe that complexity signifies sophistication or that more is always better. But in the realm of leadership and organizational design, this couldn't be further from the truth. Complexity often leads to confusion, inefficiency, and disengagement. It's time to strip away the unnecessary layers and get back to the essence of simplicity.

THE PROBLEM WITH EXCESSIVE HIERARCHIES

One of the most common culprits in organizational complexity is excessive hierarchies. Over time, businesses tend to add layers upon layers of management, believing that each new level will bring more control, more clarity, or more efficiency. However, the reality is quite the opposite. The more layers you add, the more you increase costs, miscommunication, and inefficiency.

INCREASED COSTS

Each additional layer in an organization comes with a cost. There are more salaries to pay, more people to manage, and more resources required to keep things running. According to a study by McKinsey & Company, organizations with more than five levels of hierarchy have 15% higher costs than those with fewer levels. This cost isn't just monetary; it's also in terms of time, energy, and focus that could be better spent on more productive endeavors.

Excessive layers often create a bottleneck in decision-making. Decisions that could have been made quickly by a single leader are now delayed as they need to pass through multiple levels of approval. This slow pace can frustrate employees, customers, and even the leaders themselves. It's a paradox: the more layers you have, the more difficult it becomes to make decisions, which in turn slows down progress.

MISCOMMUNICATION AND INEFFICIENCY

As organizations grow and add more layers, the lines of communication become more convoluted. Information has to pass through several levels before reaching the person who needs it. In the process, messages can get distorted, diluted, or delayed. A study by Harvard Business Review found that 80% of organizational problems stem from poor communication. When there are too many layers, it's easy for important details to slip through the cracks, leading to mistakes, confusion, and inefficiency.

Employees may also feel disconnected from the decision-making process. When leaders are too far removed from the day-to-day operations, they can lose touch with the realities that their teams face. This disconnect can lead to decisions that don't align with the needs of the workforce, further exacerbating inefficiency.

COMPLEXITY BREEDS DISTRUST AND DISENGAGEMENT

Another significant problem with excessive layers is the impact it has on trust and engagement within the organization. When employees feel like they're just one small cog in a massive machine, they often disengage. They may feel that their contributions don't matter or that their voices aren't being heard. This lack of engagement can lead to lower morale, higher turnover rates, and a general sense of dissatisfaction.

Moreover, when leaders are too far removed from their teams, it creates an atmosphere of distrust. Employees may begin to question the motives of their leaders, wondering if decisions are being made with their best interests in mind or if the leaders are simply out of touch with the reality of the work. This distrust only deepens as layers increase, creating a vicious cycle that's difficult to break.

WHY LEADERS CREATE LAYERS

Despite the many downsides of complex organizational structures, leaders often create these layers in an attempt to solve problems that don't require such drastic measures. In many cases, leaders add layers because they fear losing control.

FEAR OF LOSING CONTROL

As organizations grow, leaders often struggle with the idea of letting go of control. They may feel that if they're not involved in every decision, things will fall apart. This fear can lead them to micromanage, creating more layers to maintain oversight. However, this approach often backfires. The more control a leader tries to maintain, the more they stifle innovation, creativity, and autonomy within their teams.

In fact, research by Gallup has shown that employees who feel empowered to make decisions are 12 times more likely to be engaged in their work. When leaders hold on too tightly, they rob their teams of the opportunity to take ownership of their work, leading to disengagement and frustration.

MISGUIDED ATTEMPTS TO MICROMANAGE

Micromanagement is another common reason for the creation of unnecessary layers. Leaders may feel the need to oversee every detail of their teams' work, believing that this will ensure quality and consistency. However, micromanagement often leads to inefficiency and resentment. Employees who feel micromanaged may begin to disengage, as they feel their expertise and judgment are being undermined.

A study by the Center for Creative Leadership found that 58% of employees say they would rather work for a leader who empowers them to make decisions than one who micromanages them. Micromanagement doesn't just hinder the development of employees; it also creates unnecessary complexity in the organization. Leaders who micromanage often add layers to ensure that they can oversee every aspect of the business, which only increases the chances of miscommunication and inefficiency.

THE SOLUTION: FLATTENING STRUCTURES

So, what's the solution to the problem of excessive layers and complexity? The answer lies in flattening organizational structures. By removing unnecessary layers, organizations can streamline decision-making, improve communication, and foster a culture of trust and engagement.

BENEFITS OF LEANER ORGANIZATIONAL MODELS

Leaner organizational models have been proven to be more efficient, cost-effective, and agile. When organizations flatten their structures, they eliminate the bottlenecks that slow down decision-making. Leaders can make decisions more quickly, which allows the organization to respond to changes in the market or industry with greater flexibility.

Flattening structures also improves communication. With fewer layers, information can flow more freely between employees and leaders. This transparency helps build trust, as employees feel more connected to the decision-making process. They also feel more empowered, as they can see how their contributions directly impact the organization's success.

Moreover, leaner structures promote innovation. When employees are given more autonomy and responsibility, they are more likely to come up with creative solutions to problems. In a flatter organization, employees are encouraged to think for themselves, which fosters a sense of ownership and pride in their work.

STEPS TO STREAMLINE DECISION-MAKING AND COMMUNICATION

To flatten an organization, leaders must take several steps. The first is to assess the current structure and identify areas where layers can be removed. This may involve consolidating roles, eliminating redundant positions, or decentralizing decision-making authority.

Next, leaders should focus on improving communication. This means creating channels for open dialogue between employees and leaders, ensuring that information flows freely and efficiently. Regular check-ins, team meetings, and feedback sessions can help keep everyone on the same page.

Finally, leaders should empower their teams to make decisions. By giving employees more autonomy, leaders can foster a sense of ownership and accountability. This doesn't mean abandoning oversight entirely, but rather trusting employees to make decisions within their areas of expertise.

EXAMPLES OF SIMPLIFIED STRUCTURES

Several organizations have successfully reduced complexity by flattening their structures. One example is Zappos, the online shoe retailer. In 2014, Zappos made the bold decision to eliminate traditional management hierarchies in favor of a holacracy, a system where decision-making is distributed throughout the organization. While the transition was challenging, it ultimately led to a more agile and innovative company culture.

Another example is Google, which has long been known for its flat organizational structure. By keeping its structure lean, Google has been able to foster a culture of innovation and creativity, with employees encouraged to take risks and experiment with new ideas. This has allowed Google to stay ahead of the competition and maintain its position as a leader in the tech industry.

In the nonprofit sector, the organization Teach for America has also embraced a flatter structure. By eliminating unnecessary layers, Teach for America has been able to make quicker decisions, streamline communication, and focus on its mission of providing educational equity to underserved communities.

CONCLUSION

The cost of complexity is high, but the solution is simple: remove unnecessary layers. By flattening organizational structures, leaders can reduce costs, improve communication, and foster a culture of trust and engagement. It's time to embrace simplicity and allow your organization to thrive. As da Vinci wisely said, simplicity is the ultimate sophistication, and in leadership, that couldn't be truer.

CHAPTER 6

TOXIC MANAGERS
HOW TRUE LEADERS CAN LET GO

"People don't care how much you know until they know how much you care."

— JOHN C. MAXWELL

IDENTIFYING TOXIC LEADERSHIP

In any organization, leadership sets the tone for success or failure. Toxic managers, however, can derail even the most promising teams. Recognizing toxic leadership traits is the first step toward creating a healthier work environment. These traits often include micromanagement, favoritism, and fear-based tactics. Micromanagement stifles creativity and autonomy, leaving employees feeling disempowered. According to a study by Trinity Solutions, 79% of employees who experienced micromanagement reported decreased productivity and morale.

Favoritism is another hallmark of toxic management. When managers consistently reward a select few, it creates a divide among team members, breeding resentment and mistrust. This favoritism undermines the principle of meritocracy, leaving high-performing employees feeling undervalued.

Fear-based tactics, such as public shaming or using threats to motivate, can have an even more damaging effect. The American Psychological Association (APA) notes that fear-driven workplaces often experience higher rates of absenteeism and burnout. When employees are afraid to voice concerns or make mistakes, innovation and collaboration suffer.

THE IMPACT OF TOXICITY ON MORALE, PRODUCTIVITY, AND RETENTION

The consequences of toxic leadership extend far beyond individual grievances. A toxic manager can erode team morale, leading to a ripple effect throughout the organization. Gallup's 2022 State of the Global Workplace report revealed that 50% of employees leave their jobs specifically to escape bad managers. This statistic underscores the profound impact leadership has on retention.

Toxic environments also drain productivity. When employees are preoccupied with navigating office politics or recovering from negative interactions, they have less energy to dedicate to their work. A study by the Workplace Bullying Institute found that 30% of employees targeted by toxic behaviors experienced stress-related health issues, further reducing their ability to perform.

Retention is another critical concern. High turnover rates not only disrupt team dynamics but also incur significant financial costs. According to the Society for Human Resource Management (SHRM), replacing an employee can cost up to 200% of their annual salary. Organizations that fail to address toxic leadership risk losing their top talent to competitors, further weakening their position in the market.

THE COST OF KEEPING TOXIC MANAGERS

While some organizations may tolerate toxic managers due to their perceived performance or results, this approach often backfires. The long-term cultural damage caused by toxic leadership far outweighs any short-term gains. Toxic managers create a culture of fear and mistrust, which can be difficult to reverse. Over time, this culture becomes ingrained, making it harder to attract and retain high-quality talent.

The loss of high-performing employees is another significant cost. Talented individuals are less likely to stay in environments where they feel undervalued or unsupported. When these employees leave, they take their skills, institutional knowledge, and networks with them, leaving a void that is difficult to fill.

HOW TO ADDRESS TOXICITY

Addressing toxic leadership requires a proactive and deliberate approach. The first step is recognizing the signs early. Managers who consistently display toxic behaviors should be flagged through regular performance reviews and anonymous employee feedback. Surveys and 360-degree feedback mechanisms can provide valuable insights into managerial effectiveness and areas for improvement.

Once toxic behaviors are identified, organizations must provide opportunities for improvement. This can include targeted training programs, mentorship, and coaching. For example, emotional intelligence training has been shown to improve managerial performance significantly. A study published in the Journal of Applied Psychology found that leaders with high emotional intelligence foster more positive work environments and achieve better team outcomes.

However, not all toxic managers are willing or able to change. In such cases, it is crucial to remove them from their roles. While this decision may be difficult, it is often necessary to protect the organization's culture and long-term success. Transparency during this process is key. Clearly communicate the reasons for the decision and emphasize the organization's commitment to fostering a positive workplace.

BUILDING A POSITIVE LEADERSHIP CULTURE

The ultimate goal is to create a culture that not only discourages toxic behaviors but actively promotes positive leadership. This begins with recruiting and promoting leaders who align with the organization's values. During the hiring process, assess candidates' leadership styles and their ability to inspire and support their teams. Behavioral interview questions and reference checks can help identify candidates who prioritize collaboration and empathy.

Promoting from within can also be an effective strategy. Employees who have demonstrated strong interpersonal skills and a commitment to the company's mission are often well-suited for leadership roles. Providing leadership development programs can further prepare these individuals for success.

Organizations should also establish clear expectations for leadership behavior. This includes defining core values and incorporating them into performance evaluations. Leaders should be held accountable for their actions and rewarded for fostering positive team dynamics. For example, Google's Project Oxygen identified key behaviors of effective managers, such as empowering teams, expressing interest in employees' well-being, and being a good communicator. By prioritizing these traits, organizations can cultivate a culture of trust and mutual respect.

Finally, ongoing support and development are essential. Leadership is a skill that requires continuous learning and adaptation. Providing access to resources, such as workshops, seminars, and peer networks, can help leaders stay informed and effective. Encouraging open communication and feedback ensures that issues are addressed promptly and constructively.

CONCLUSION

Toxic managers are a significant barrier to organizational success, but they are not an insurmountable one. By identifying toxic traits, addressing harmful behaviors, and fostering a culture of positive leadership, organizations can create environments where employees thrive. As Simon Sinek's quote reminds us, true leadership is about taking care of those in your charge. When leaders prioritize the well-being and growth of their teams, the entire organization benefits.

CHAPTER 7

THE POWER OF SIMPLIFIED LEADERSHIP

"Perfection is achieved, not when there is nothing more to add, but when there is nothing left to take away."

— ANTOINE DE SAINT-EXUPÉRY

In an era dominated by complexity, where every decision feels layered with unnecessary steps, simplified leadership emerges as a breath of fresh air. It is not about cutting corners or oversimplifying the intricacies of running a business. Instead, it is about stripping away the noise, focusing on what truly matters, and leading with clarity and purpose. Simplified leadership is an approach that prioritizes trust, respect, empathy, and service—the core values that form the foundation of authentic and impactful leadership.

WHAT SIMPLIFIED LEADERSHIP LOOKS LIKE

At its heart, simplified leadership is built on a few essential principles that guide every decision and interaction:

Core Values: Trust, Respect, Empathy, and Service

Simplified leadership thrives on trust. According to a 2022 study by Edelman, 88% of employees believe trust in their leaders is critical for workplace satisfaction. Respect and empathy go hand in hand, fostering a culture where employees feel valued and understood. Service—the act of putting the needs of others first—rounds out the core values. Leaders who serve their teams create environments where collaboration and innovation flourish.

Prioritizing People Over Processes

While processes provide structure, it is the people who drive results. Simplified leadership focuses on empowering individuals rather than being bogged down by rigid systems. Take, for instance, the approach of Satya Nadella, CEO of Microsoft, who transformed the company by shifting its culture from one of competition to one of collaboration. By emphasizing empathy and learning, Nadella prioritized his people, leading Microsoft to regain its position as one of the most valuable companies in the world.

KEY BENEFITS OF SIMPLICITY

The benefits of simplified leadership are profound, impacting not just the organization but also the individuals within it. Here are a few key advantages:

Improved Efficiency and Productivity

Complexity often leads to confusion and wasted resources. A 2018 study by McKinsey & Company found that organizations that streamlined their operations saw a 20-30% improvement in productivity. Simplified leadership ensures that teams are aligned, with clear goals and minimal distractions, allowing them to work smarter, not harder.

Enhanced Team Satisfaction

When leaders focus on simplicity, they create environments where employees feel less overwhelmed and more engaged. Gallup's 2021 State of the Global Workplace report revealed that only 20% of employees are engaged at work. Simplified leadership—with its emphasis on clarity and purpose—can significantly boost this figure by addressing the root causes of disengagement.

Adaptability in a Rapidly Changing Business Environment

In today's fast-paced world, businesses that can adapt quickly have a distinct advantage. Simplified leadership fosters agility by eliminating bureaucratic hurdles and empowering teams to make decisions swiftly. Consider how Airbnb navigated the challenges of the COVID-19 pandemic. By simplifying its operations and focusing on its core mission—providing unique travel experiences—the company not only survived but thrived, achieving record profitability in 2021.

IMPLEMENTING SIMPLIFIED LEADERSHIP

While the benefits are clear, the journey to adopting simplified leadership requires intentional effort. Here are practical steps to get started:

Setting Clear Priorities and Eliminating Distractions

Simplified leadership begins with clarity. Leaders must identify the organization's top priorities and communicate them effectively. According to the Harvard Business Review, leaders who articulate clear priorities are 70% more likely to achieve their goals. Eliminating distractions—whether it's unnecessary meetings or redundant processes—frees up time and energy for what truly matters.

Encouraging Autonomy and Accountability

Empowering employees to take ownership of their work is a cornerstone of simplified leadership. A 2020 report by Deloitte found that organizations with high levels of autonomy saw a 33% increase in innovation. By trusting their teams and holding them accountable for results, leaders create a culture of ownership and initiative.

SUCCESS STORIES

The impact of simplified leadership is best illustrated through real-world examples:

Alan Mulally at Ford Motor Company

When Alan Mulally took over as CEO of Ford in 2006, the company was on the brink of bankruptcy. Mulally implemented a simplified leadership approach, focusing on transparency, teamwork, and a clear vision. By eliminating silos and fostering collaboration, he turned Ford around, leading it to record profits by 2010.

Indra Nooyi at PepsiCo

As CEO of PepsiCo, Indra Nooyi simplified the company's strategy by focusing on "Performance with Purpose." She prioritized sustainability and health-conscious products while maintaining financial performance. Her leadership not only boosted the company's reputation but also resulted in a 78% increase in shareholder value during her tenure.

Elon Musk at SpaceX

Elon Musk's leadership at SpaceX is another testament to the power of simplicity. By focusing on a single mission—making space exploration affordable and sustainable—Musk streamlined operations and inspired his team to achieve groundbreaking milestones, such as the successful launch and landing of reusable rockets.

FINAL THOUGHTS

Simplified leadership is not a one-size-fits-all approach. It requires leaders to adapt its principles to their unique contexts, always keeping the core values of trust, respect, empathy, and service at the forefront. By prioritizing people over processes, setting clear priorities, and fostering autonomy, leaders can unlock the full potential of their teams and organizations.

As you reflect on your own leadership journey, consider this: What can you simplify today to lead with greater impact tomorrow? The answer may be simpler than you think.

CONCLUSION

EMBRACING A LIFE OF PURPOSE AND JOY

As we come to the conclusion of this journey, let me remind you of a simple yet profound truth: your life is a gift, and how you choose to live it matters not only to you but to those around you. The essence of everything we've discussed boils down to one fundamental idea—keep it simple. Simplicity, in thought and action, has the power to transform lives, organizations, and communities.

Think about it: medicine can keep you stress-free for a few hours, and substances like dope might give you temporary highs. But nothing compares to the joy and fulfillment that come from harnessing the natural dopamine your body produces. By disciplining your mind, practicing self-awareness, and embracing gratitude, you can unlock a level of happiness that no external substance can replicate. The key lies within you.

DISCIPLINE YOUR MIND

The journey to happiness begins with taking control of your thoughts. Discipline your mind through practices like self-talk, meditation, and connecting with a power greater than yourself. For some, that power might be God; for others, it could be the vast and mysterious universe. Whatever you believe in, take time to reflect and seek guidance from this higher power. If you've ever doubted the existence of such a force, close your eyes and ask for clarity. Trust me, you'll begin to sense a guiding voice that will lead you toward your purpose.

When I was 12 years old, I became an orphan. It was a time filled with uncertainty and challenges. Yet, even in those dark moments, I believed in something greater than myself. That belief gave me the strength to persevere and the courage to dream. Today, as you read these words, I hope my experiences inspire you to believe in your own potential. If an orphaned boy can find his way, so can you.

THE POWER OF FAITH AND GRATITUDE

Faith has been a cornerstone of my life. It's what kept me going when the odds were stacked against me. But faith alone isn't enough; it must be paired with gratitude. Gratitude shifts your focus from what you lack to what you have. It's a practice that can transform your perspective and, ultimately, your life.

I've often said that love is infinite. The more you give, the more you receive. Love and gratitude go hand in hand, creating a cycle of joy and fulfillment. When you approach life with an attitude of gratitude, you'll find that even the simplest things—a smile, a kind word, or a moment of peace— become sources of immense joy.

LEADERSHIP AND INTEGRITY

In the world of business and leadership, integrity is non-negotiable. A value-driven culture promotes honesty, transparency, and good behavior.

Leaders who embody these principles inspire trust and commitment among their teams. Conversely, when leaders fail to align their actions with their words, they undermine organizational culture and erode trust.

I've observed that the most successful organizations invest in people. They prioritize leadership development, encourage self-improvement, and foster a culture of learning. Reading biographies of great leaders and studying their journeys can provide valuable insights into what it takes to lead with purpose and authenticity.

As a leader, you must ask yourself tough questions: Are my actions aligned with my values? Am I fostering an environment of trust and respect? Remember, insincere flattery and pretense can only take you so far. True leadership is about serving others and lifting them up.

THE ELEPHANT IN THE ROOM

One of the most challenging aspects of leadership is addressing the "elephant in the room"—the disconnect between stated values and actual practices. When organizations fail to confront this reality, they risk losing the trust and respect of their employees. The foundation of any successful organization is built on trust. Without it, even the most ambitious visions will crumble.

To create a thriving workplace, leaders must prioritize honesty and openness. Trusted employees are happier, more productive, and more committed. This, in turn, leads to better products, services, and customer satisfaction. It's a simple equation: happy employees equal happy customers.

The Role of Family and Legacy

As you reflect on your journey, consider the legacy you want to leave behind. What will people remember about you? What impact will you have on your family, friends, and community? These are questions worth pondering.

It's natural to want to provide for your loved ones, but too much material wealth can sometimes do more harm than good. Instead of focusing solely on financial inheritance, invest in your family's emotional and intellectual growth. Teach them the values of love, honesty, and respect. Encourage them to read, learn, and explore their true potential.

I've seen families torn apart by greed and entitlement. Don't let that be your story. Provide your children with the tools they need to lead meaningful lives. Help them understand that true happiness comes from within, not from external possessions.

Coping with Challenges

Life is full of challenges, but it's in these difficult moments that we grow the most. The darker it gets, the brighter the light will seem when you emerge on the other side. Every setback is an opportunity to learn, adapt, and become stronger.

When I lost my mother at a young age, I could have easily gone down a destructive path. But the seeds of faith and resilience she planted in me kept me grounded. Her blessings and teachings became my guiding light, reminding me that I was destined for more. You, too, have the power to overcome adversity. Trust in your journey and keep moving forward.

THE IMPORTANCE OF SELF-AWARENESS

Self-awareness is the foundation of a fulfilling life. It's about understanding who you are, what you value, and what brings you joy. Ask yourself questions like: Who am I? What is my purpose? What does happiness mean to me? These questions may not have immediate answers, but the act of asking them will set you on a path of discovery.

If you're fortunate enough to have a life partner, take the time to truly know them. Building a strong, loving relationship requires effort and self-awareness. When you're happy at home, that happiness spills over into every other aspect of your life.

LIVING A BALANCED LIFE

Balance is key to a happy and healthy life. It's about finding harmony between work, family, and personal growth. While work is important, it shouldn't come at the expense of your well-being or relationships. Spend quality time with your loved ones, nurture your passions, and take care of your body and mind. My wife, Catherine, and my daughter, Josephine, have been a constant reminder of the importance of cherishing family bonds. Their unwavering love and support have inspired me to prioritize balance and harmony in life.

Your body is a gift from your creator, fully equipped to sustain you. Treat it with respect. Stay active, eat well, and prioritize mental health. Laughter, meditation, and gratitude are powerful tools for maintaining balance and activating your body's natural happiness hormones.

MONEY AND HAPPINESS

Let's talk about money. While it's true that money can't buy happiness, it's also true that financial stability is important. The key is to let money serve you, not the other way around. Focus on earning money in ways that align with your values and bring you joy. Use it to create positive experiences and help others.

Remember, the quality of time you spend with your family is more important than the quantity of money you leave behind. Teach your children to value experiences, relationships, and personal growth over material possessions.

THE POWER OF LOVE AND KINDNESS

Love is the most powerful force in the universe. It's infinite, abundant, and transformative. The more you give, the more you receive. By practicing love and kindness, you'll create a ripple effect that touches everyone around you.

Kindness doesn't have to be grand or dramatic. It can be as simple as a smile, a kind word, or a helping hand. These small acts of love have the power to change lives and create a better world.

EMBRACING YOUR PURPOSE

Your purpose is unique to you. It's the reason you're here, the mission you were created to fulfill. Don't leave this world without discovering and embracing it. Your purpose will bring you happiness, fulfillment, and peace.

If you're unsure of your purpose, start by being present. Meditate, reflect, and listen to that small, guiding voice within you. It will lead you in the right direction. Trust in the journey and have faith that you're exactly where you're meant to be.

FINAL THOUGHTS

As we part ways, I want you to know that you have the power to create a life of joy, purpose, and abundance. Whether you're a leader in your organization, a parent raising the next generation, or someone searching for meaning, the principles we've discussed can guide you toward a fulfilling life.

Remember, happiness starts from within. Discipline your mind, practice gratitude, and embrace love and kindness. Invest in your growth and the growth of those around you. And most importantly, keep it simple.

Thank you for allowing me to share my journey and insights with you. I hope these words inspire you to live a life of purpose and joy. Whether I'm here on Earth or watching from above, know that my greatest happiness comes from seeing you thrive.

Until we meet again, stay true to yourself, cherish your loved ones, and never stop seeking the light. The world is a better place because you're in it.

With love and gratitude,

Fidel